#StartOutSmart

What Every Entrepreneur
Needs to Know Now, Not Later

Waukeshia D. Jackson, Esq.

Contact the author:

www.jllawgroup.com

All social media: @JLLawGroup

ISBN: 978-1542568760

First Edition January 2017

"Before reading #StartOutSmart, everything I learned about being an entrepreneur and protecting my business name and brand, I learned from the internet. I can honestly say after reading this book, I am better for it and will be making some changes and updates. It's clear and concise. I wish I had it in the beginning.

Juanita Patterson, Owner - JRP Events

"Working with Ms. Jackson has truly been an enlightening process. She talks about the technical process of patents in a way that a layperson would understand. Reading this book StartOutSmart will be a huge help to all who want to learn how to navigate the legal processes associated with starting a business."

Nicole Hickman, Founder- Egami Media, LLC

"Waukeshia D. Jackson is an impeccable attorney. She gives advice that is concise and easy to understand. As an entrepreneur, it is critical that I establish a solid legal foundation for my business. Waukeshia facilitates this process by interpreting any legal language and explaining exactly how it would impact me and my business."

Tijuana Mesidor, Owner – Vibrant Phase Photography

"I think that #StartOutSmart is the best place to start for anyone starting a business. This book provides educational, reliable, and easy-to-read information. Also, this book is a well written resource that is extremely useful for non-attorney audiences. "

Carla Hogan, Owner – Sweet Elegance by Carla

<u>Dedication</u>

I would like to dedicate this book to my Aunt Dot who challenged me, inspired me, encouraged me, supported me and prayed for me along the way. I always tried my best to make sure that you knew your value to me. Please continue to watch over me from heaven.

TABLE OF CONTENTS

« CHAPTER ONE »

Introduction

Let me start by answering two questions that I am often asked by entrepreneurs. First, what is intellectual property? Second, why should I care about protecting it? Think of intellectual property as a commercial asset like a building or piece of property that can be licensed, bought and sold. The purpose of protecting your intellectual property is to prevent other people, businesses, and competitors from copying your innovative efforts.

Entrepreneurs often ask why they should care about protecting their intellectual property. My response is always the same; if it is worth stealing then it's probably worth protecting. Intellectual property can make or break a startup business. Once someone else takes your name, idea, or product, recovering it is a process that can be costly. So, if you think you have come up with an idea that is going to make you a lot of money, then you may want to have something in place to protect it.

Intellectual property is essentially a business tool. You have to protect it, you have to enforce it, and you have to maintain it. So before you spend money getting a patent or getting a trademark or trying to put particular agreements in place, be sure to understand what particular business objective this is serving. From my experience, entrepreneurs just starting out in their business go in either one of two directions when it comes to protecting their intellectual property. They either: (1) go too far in terms of protecting themselves which largely impacts their pockets or (2) totally avoid legal protection altogether because it is costly, confusing or they don't know what to do or where to start.

You love your brand and you love your business and are probably passionate about it. If you have a truly unique product, system or brand weigh the pros and cons of protecting it legally. Protecting your intellectual property may not seem big initially, but the larger you grow and the larger your business grows, the more people may want to copy your idea and profit from your hard work.

Another consideration for entrepreneurs, small businesses, and startup companies, is that almost all of the big companies are no longer spending the time and money in research and development. Instead, they wait for smaller companies to do the innovation and then once the smaller companies prove that there is a market for the new innovative product, idea, or system, then the larger company buys the smaller company or startup which includes the intellectual property that the smaller company may own.

In most cases, the value of an early-stage business is based primarily on its intellectual property, such as its rights in inventions, literary and artistic works, and the symbols, images, and names used to identify the business to its prospective customers. Whether you are in the dream phase of your business or in the launch phase of your startup, remember if you start out early and put in the time, effort, and money to get intellectual property protection at the outset, your brand may be stronger. Your investors will have peace of mind and you will have exclusive rights to profit from the unique ideas, systems, products, or brands that you have created.

* * *

« CHAPTER TWO »

Non-Disclosure/Confidentiality Agreements

Should I use a non-disclosure agreement ("NDA") or not is often a question that a lot of entrepreneurs wrestle with starting out. Let's say you have an idea. You may need to talk with someone about funding or developing your idea. For example, when you are out looking for investors in your company or business, people might decide that they like your idea but that they, in fact don't like you. (Let's be honest, it happens.) What should you do? You can either file a provisional patent application (discussed in Chapter 2) or you can put a non-disclosure agreement in place. If you have to disclose any information about your new idea to anyone, at the very least you should make sure that you have a non-disclosure or confidentiality agreement in place.

Why? To answer that, let's consider the definition and purpose of a non-disclosure agreement. Basically, a NDA is an agreement that states whenever you are sharing your business idea with other people, those individuals cannot then share the information regarding your business idea with other people or start the business themselves.

Think about it, trade secrets, confidential information, and business "know how" are often some of the most valuable forms of intellectual property for most businesses. However, if any of these forms of intellectual property are disclosed to another party without proper contractual or legal protection mechanisms in place, then the rights to these trade secrets, confidential information, and business "know-how" are lost. This means that as an entrepreneur you cannot stop other people from using them.

Therefore, there are several key issues to consider in ensuring that your NDA is enforceable. In general, a proper NDA should clearly define what is considered confidential information, and moreover, what is **NOT** considered confidential information. Usually an NDA defines that any information relating to products, services, markets, customers, research, software, developments, inventions, designs, drawings, financials, and other items, is to be kept confidential. Some examples of things that are NOT typically considered confidential information may include information already in possession of the receiving party or information that is already known to the public.

As a practical matter, business owners should always make sure that confidential information is labeled or marked confidential. As an entrepreneur, you may also want to follow-up in meetings where your idea is discussed and make sure that you make a list of things that were confidential and subject to the NDA and send the list to the meeting participants. Also, NEVER sign a NDA that does not specifically indicate what is considered confidential information, as you don't want the courts to interpret the definition for you.

When using an NDA, another question to ask is whether the agreement should protect the information of both parties or just one party. For example, if it is just you disclosing information then there should be a one way NDA or confidentiality agreement that protects only your information. You can think of a one-way NDA as protecting your information, but not the information of the other party. However, in a two-way or mutual NDA, both parties are on the hook for maintaining the confidentiality of the information presented.

Another key element to negotiate in an NDA is the 'Term' of the agreement. You can think of the term as how long the confidential information will be protected. For example, most NDA's have a provision to maintain secrecy for a specific time period, for example: 1 year, 3 years, 5 years, 7 years, etc. However, once the time period that has been set for the term of the NDA passes or expires, the other party no longer has an obligation to keep any of the information secret, which means that they can use it and you can't stop them. Rather than put in a specific number of years, you may want to ensure that the obligation to keep the information secret continues until the information becomes available to the general public and readily accessible.

One downside to using a NDA to protect your ideas, confidential information or intellectual property, is that when the terms of the non-disclosure agreement are violated, the only solution that the entrepreneur has is to sue and seek for a remedy under contract law which can cost an upwards of $100,000. So it is important to ask yourself if someone signs your NDA, and steals your idea what you are going to do. Are you going to take them to court? If you have deep pockets, then go for it. Otherwise, NDA's are typically more effective for companies that have deep pockets and teams of lawyers to help them to enforce these agreements.

Another downside is that most investors will not sign a NDA. Investors are often presented with so many ideas that if they sign a NDA with one entrepreneur or inventor they will not be able to work with any other companies that might be doing the same or similar thing.

Key Takeaways

- Having a signed NDA agreement in place gives the entrepreneur or small business owner the confidence that the party that they are working with will maintain the confidentiality of their information, trade secrets and business "know how".

- Enforcing a NDA can be expensive.

- NDAs should not be used as the sole means of protecting your intellectual property.

« CHAPTER THREE »

Patents

Quite often, entrepreneurs confuse patents with trademarks and copyrights. To be clear, you can't patent expressions like books, writings, drawings, and music, these things are protected by copyrights. Likewise, you can't patent brand names, logos, and slogans, these things are protected by trademarks. Patents, on the other hand, protect new, useful and non-obvious inventions.

Patents, like all other forms of intellectual property, begin with an idea. With the success of the American television series Shark Tank, budding entrepreneurs are constantly asking if they should obtain a patent. Generally speaking, entrepreneurs are inventors by nature, and no one wants to have their idea or invention stolen. So what can you do as an entrepreneur to protect your ideas and inventions? If patent protection is available, just having filed for a patent prior to disclosing the idea to a company will put you in a much better position than simply having an NDA or confidentiality agreement.

Patents are basically legally binding "dibs" on your inventions. There are actually 3 types of patents in the United States:

- Utility patent – (protects the functional features of your invention)
- Design patent – (protects the appearance of your invention)
- Plant patent – (protects discoveries and reproductions of new varieties of plants)

The utility patent is probably the most important category of patents, and it is typically what people refer to when they discuss patents in general. For the purpose of this book, the use of the term "patent" refers to the utility patent.

If you have an invention and you apply for and obtain a patent from the United States Patent and Trademark ("USPTO") you can create barriers of entry to individuals, businesses and competitors operating in your industry. It is often a common misconception among entrepreneurs that obtaining a patent in the United States gives you the right to make, sell, or use your invention. This is **NOT** the case. A patent gives you the right to stop others from making, selling, using or offering for sale your invention in the United States. Having a patent will grant you this right for a period of 20 years from the date that you originally filed your patent application.

Although patents are absolutely essential to business, patents are also the most expensive and the most difficult pieces of intellectual property to obtain. Generally, the cost for a nonprovisional patent application is between 8 thousand ($8.000) and 15 thousand ($15,000) dollars (not including maintenance fees, issue fees, and examination costs), and patents typically require the assistance of a patent attorney. It is important for entrepreneurs to keep in mind that these costs are for getting a patent in the United States. Getting a patent in other countries requires even more fees. Additionally, the timeframe between filing a patent application and obtaining an issued patent can take years primarily because the United States Patent and Trademark Office typically rejects initial patent applications which often requires the inventor to go back and forth with the USPTO. This process takes more time and also costs more money.

More importantly, the United States is now a first to file system for filing patent applications meaning you have to file your patent application before anybody else. In order to get your patent application on file with the United States Patent and Trademark Office, you can file what is called a provisional patent application in order to quickly protect your invention. A provisional patent application lasts for 12 months and allows you to communicate to the USPTO that this is your invention while giving you additional time to conduct further research and to market your invention. However, it is important to bear in mind that the 12-month pendency of a provisional patent application cannot be extended.

A provisional application will never issue as a patent. In order to get a patent, you will eventually have to convert the provisional application to a nonprovisional patent application. However, filing a provisional patent application may be used as a beginning step in the patent process and costs much less than filing a nonprovisional application. For example, costs for filing a provisional patent application typically range between 5 thousand ($5,000) and 8 thousand ($8,000) dollars. Provisional patent applications have fewer filing requirements than nonprovisional patent applications which is the primary reason that the cost for preparing a provisional patent application is significantly lower than the costs associated with filing a nonprovisional patent application.

Moreover, filing a provisional patent application will establish your priority date and can prevent others from attempting to patent the invention themselves. Although a provisional patent application never matures into an issued patent, filing a provisional patent application gives you patent pending status. It also preserves your priority date or filing date. So that if you later file a nonprovisional patent application (that claims the benefit of your provisional patent application) within 12 months after filing a provisional, it acts as if the nonprovisional was filed on the same date as the provisional patent application.

* * *

Key Takeaways

- Consult with a patent attorney or patent agent to determine if your idea is patentable.

- Assuming your idea is patentable, file a provisional patent application before you disclose your idea to other people.

- File your patent application before someone else does.

« CHAPTER FOUR »

Trademarks and Service Marks

What is a trademark? Technically, trademarks identify the source of goods. Service marks identify the source of services. However, people use the term trademarks to refer to both trademarks and service marks. A trademark can be a word, symbol, logo, slogan, color, scent, sound, design, or combination of these used to distinguish or identify goods and services of one company or individual from the goods and services of other companies or individuals.

The main point of a trademark is to keep down confusion. Trademarks help to keep consumers from being misled by directing consumers to the goods or service that they want. As a result, trademarks give you the exclusive right to prevent other people, businesses, competitors from using the same or similar mark that may cause consumers (clients, customers, etc.) to be confused about whose goods and/or services they are buying.

This does not mean that a trademark owner owns the mark in all contexts. For example, anyone can use the words "blackberry" to describe an edible berry fruit that is dark in color. Or use the word "blackberry" to sell something completely unrelated to electronic mobile devices like candy. But any use of the word "blackberry" to sell mobile telephones, personal data assistants, and computer related technology devices and you are likely to be completely shut down by Blackberry Inc. Additionally, you would probably have to pay Blackberry Inc. large amounts of money, stop using the "blackberry" mark with computers or similar technology, and completely destroy any and all products that contain the mark.

Assuming that your business is using or has intentions to use a mark as a trademark, then you should register your logo or other marks for your business as soon as possible. Generally speaking, the sooner you can get trademark protection for your business the better. With trademarks, entrepreneurs can protect the names of the businesses that they create.

However, a common misconception is that people often think that if they have registered their business name with the Secretary of State's office then that means that they also are entitled to or have the rights to a trademark for that name. Unfortunately, that's not how the trademark process works. A business name is simply a name under which you do business in a particular state. A business name registration does not give you trademark rights. In order to have trademark rights, you must use your mark in commerce. By simply being the first person to use your mark in your area, you could potentially have rights to use your mark in your area and also prohibit others from using your mark in your area. This is called common law rights and does not require paying any fees or filing formal filing documents with a government agency.

However, if you want protection for your mark nationally you must file an application for trademark registration with the United States Patent and Trademark Office ("USPTO"). What this means is that you **CAN** get limited trademark rights simply by going into business under a distinctive name. Through common law trademark rights, entrepreneurs can basically get rights to trademarks on a first come, first served basis. However, the common law rights only extend to the geographic area in which you are using your trademark. Put another way, common law rights allow you the right to sue another party for infringement assuming that you can prove that you started using the trademark in your particular area before they did.

You can also register your trademark with your state. Doing so will allow you to have rights to use your trademark **solely** within that particular state. Although the process for registering a trademark with the state is less rigorous than applying for a federally registered mark, the fees associated with obtaining a state trademark can be equally as costly as obtaining a federal registration. And, state trademarks generally provide far less legal protection than federal trademarks.

Alternatively, a business operating in more than one state may file for a federal trademark. A federal registered trademark gives you a presumption of ownership in the trademark and rights to use the mark throughout the entire United States and its territories.

Before choosing a name for your business, a logo design, slogan, etc. that you would like to trademark, it is important to do a trademark search to determine whether or not the name you are considering is currently being used by someone else. If you have already adopted and used a product or service trademark, it may be wise to have a search done to discover potential conflicts with other trademark owners. This can help you make an educated decision about continued use of your trademark, before any issues arise. Although you can perform a basic search yourself using the Trademark Electronic Search System, it is better to contact a trademark attorney to get a more comprehensive search.

Generally speaking, you should engage the services of an experienced trademark attorney if you are starting a new business or whenever your company is considering launching a new product or service. The best time to get a trademark attorney involved is before you have committed significant resources and money to a particular name, logo design, or other mark. To this end, entrepreneurs often question the value or benefit of obtaining an attorney at this stage because they feel that they can simply perform a trademark search themselves. Although this is true, an experienced trademark attorney can help you avoid costly mistakes in the selection and use of your product or service trademark, as well as, advise you of the risks associated with trademark use, review and evaluate the results of a trademark search, and assist you in adopting and choosing a mark that reduces your risks.

Moreover, when selecting a trademark, the mark needs to be DRAMATIC and memorable. The best trademarks are marks or words that have absolutely nothing to do with your business or made up words. For example, brands such as Pepsi®, Kodak®, Starbucks®, Verizon®, Xerox® and Reebok® have been created for the sole purpose of functioning as a trademark and have no other meaning other than acting as a trademark..

It is also important to note that your business name, slogan, logo, domain name and design are all separate trademarks. Meaning, your business name and your logo are separate trademarks even if your business name is incorporated within the logo. Therefore, each of these must be trademarked separately if you intend to use them separately. Another important thing to keep in mind is that each application will incur its own fees and costs.

After you have a trademark, whether you have a common law trademark or a federally registered trademark, it is imperative to put people on notice that you have acquired trademark rights in a new mark or logo. In order to do this, you simply add ™ to the end of your mark for common law trademarks. For federally registered trademarks, you would use ® at the end of your mark. Using these indicators sends a message to other people, businesses and competitors that you are serious about the use of your trademark. It is also important to note, however, that use of the ® without federally registering your mark with the USPTO is a crime under the laws of the United States.

Once you have obtained a U.S federal trademark registration, you must take certain steps to maintain the registration. Otherwise the USPTO will cancel your trademark registration. Specifically, there are two separate steps involved in maintaining your trademark registration. First, you must show use of your trademark no later than the 6th year after it is registered, then again before the 10th year, and then again every 10 years after that. Secondly, you must renew your trademark registration. This must be done every 10 years. The dates for renewal are critical. If you ignore them, the USPTO can simply cancel your registration. The USPTO will **NOT** notify you that a filing is due. It is your sole responsibility to remember this date. All renewal dates are measured from the date that your trademark registration was issued—not from the date you filed the application.   Unfortunately, this step is often overlooked and forgotten by most entrepreneurs. Consequently, there is a large group of individuals, entrepreneurs and small business owners that think that they have a trademark, when in fact they do not.

Key Takeaways

- Do a trademark search prior to choosing a mark.

- Choose a name that is DRAMATIC, DISTINCTIVE, and MEMORABLE.

- Make sure to use your mark continuously.

- Renew your mark to avoid cancellation.

« CHAPTER FIVE »

Trade Secrets

As an emerging entrepreneur, startup company, or small business owner, it is imperative to take the steps necessary to protect your technology and your brand. Generally, emerging businesses will consider protecting their intellectual property with either patents or trade secrets. Choosing to invest some resources into obtaining intellectual property protection can be a tremendous decision. If you decide that you do not want to pursue patent protection because either it is too expensive or your invention is not the right type of subject matter that is typically protected by patents, then you may want to protect your idea using trade secrets. To this end, it is critical to consider the basic types of intellectual property protection that trade secrets provide.

Many successful businesses often have very valuable secrets such as, business plans, processes, formulas, source code, product designs, customer lists, vendor lists, and algorithms which **ALL** can be considered trade secrets. While there are no formal filing requirements for protecting your secret information as a trade secret, in order for a business's secret to be afforded legal protection as a trade secret, there are typically three factors to consider: (1) the secret information must provide an economic benefit to your business; (2) the secret information must not be generally known by others, and (3) you must take reasonable steps to keep the information secret. The critical requirement for trade secret protection lies in maintaining the secrecy of the information. Consequently, trade secrets can last for as long as you like as long as you keep the information secret. Methods or information revealed to the public cannot be protected under trade secret laws. To this end, judges require that you take affirmative steps to keep your secret information – secret. Therefore, you should set up policies and procedures to protect them. Such policies may include the following:

- Ensure that everyone who sees your secret information knows that it is secret. Mark and label material as proprietary and confidential. Have them to sign non-disclosure agreements prior to sharing your secret information with them.

- Secure and lock up your secret information. Lock doors, hire security guards, put up gates, signs, fences, etc.

- Use employee and visitor identification badges to control access to your business. Do not leave confidential information lying around and exposed when you have visitors.

- Set up encryption. Set up passwords. Require employees to keep their computer systems locked when they are away from their desks or offices.

- Take measures to ensure that employees who leave your business regardless of how they were terminated do not leave with sensitive information.

On the other hand, the downside to protecting your secret information with a trade secret is that trade secrets can potentially be figured out by other people, businesses, or even competitors through reverse engineering. Meaning if other people become aware of your trade secrets on their own or through information available to the public, then they are free to use the information and there is nothing that you can do to stop them.

Therefore, there are some factors to consider when choosing to protect your intellectual property with trade secrets:

(1) Will you need intellectual property protection to last beyond 20 years?

(2) Is your invention something that can easily be reverse engineered?

Key Takeaways

- A trade secret is information that is valuable because it is kept secret.

- State laws prevent the "misappropriation" of trade secrets. This basically means that people aren't allowed to steal your secret information.

- Other people can independently create or reverse engineer your trade secrets.

« CHAPTER SIX »

Copyrights

The form of intellectual property protection easiest for many small business owners, entrepreneurs and startups to understand is copyright protection. Copyright law prevents others from taking or copying your work without paying for it. Copyright law also prevents others from altering the work you created without your permission.

In a nutshell, Copyright law protects the "original works of authorship" fixed in a tangible medium of expression. What this means is that in order to obtain copyright protection the work must be original or independently created and not copied from someone else's work. Also, the work must be fixed such as digitally saved or stored or written on a piece of paper. For example, Copyright law protects things such as, pictures, books, films, songs and software.

Copyright is a very easy, inexpensive, and yet, extremely powerful right to obtain. For one thing a copyright lasts for an extremely long time. Generally speaking, copyrights last the life of the author plus 70 years. Copyrights owned or created by a corporation for example using a work for hire doctrine last from the date of creation plus 120 years or date of publication plus 95 years whichever is shorter.

Not to mention, a copyright is created automatically each and every time an original work is fixed in a tangible medium. That is to say that once you have created an original work it is instantly protected under Copyright law. Once you have created your work you may want to put others on notice of your ownership in the copyright of the work. Although the use of a copyright notice is no longer required under the laws of the United States, the use of copyright notice is still important because it informs everyone that the work is protected by copyright, identifies the copyright owner, and shows the year in which the copyright was first published.

A copyright notice should contain the following elements:

- The symbol © (the letter "C" in a circle), or the word "Copyright" or the abbreviation "Copr."
- The year of first publication of the work
- The name of the copyright owner.

Example: © 2017 Jane Doe

Like trademarks, you do not have to formally register your copyright or pay a fee in order to have legal protection under U.S. Copyright law. However, if you intend to commercially exploit or make money from your work then you may want to consider registering your work with the U.S. Copyright Office. Formal registration with the U.S. Copyright Office increases your ability to enforce your rights to your work. Although there are several benefits to formally registering your work, the biggest benefit is that you can **NOT** bring a lawsuit against someone who infringes your copyright **UNTIL** after you formally register with the

U.S. Copyright Office. Put another way, you must register your copyright **FIRST** otherwise you cannot file a lawsuit.

You can register your copyright simply by visiting the Copyright Office's website (www.copyright.gov) and either filing for copyright registration electronically or by completing the paper form. .Filing electronically is typically cheaper that filing a paper application. For example, fees for electronically filing your copyright registration are approximately $35.00 or $55.00 depending on the circumstances. While the fees for paper filings are approximately $85.00. Additionally, the Copyright Office typically processes electronic filings within 3-5 months. While the processing time for paper filings typically takes 7-13 months. It is also important to point out that the effective date of your registration is the date that he Copyright Office receives your completed application.

In addition, formal registration of your work with the U.S. Copyright Office provides constructive notice to everyone that you own the copyrighted work making it harder for others to claim that they infringed the work unknowingly. Not to mention, registration is evidence that you are indeed the actual owner of the copyright.

Also, is important to realize that you can register your work at any time, but there are benefits to registering your work before or shortly after publication, and definitely prior to infringement. Specifically, copyright registration should occur within three (3) months of the work's publication date or before any copyright infringement actually begins. Registration of your work within this time frame typically makes it much easier to sue and recover damages (money) from someone who infringes your work. To this end, timely registration allows you to recover up to $150,000 per work and possibly attorneys' fees making it more likely that you can retain a lawyer on a contingency fee basis. Therefore, copyrights are an extremely powerful and potentially valuable form of intellectual property.

Additionally, registration of your work with the Copyright Office may make it easier to transfer your copyright. In fact, in some industries copyright registration is a prerequisite to get people to take you seriously. Thus, it is a good business practice to register your work as soon as possible after it has been created.

The real power of copyright protection lies in the exclusivity of rights it provides to the owner. Meaning as the creator of your work, you and only you will have the right to control what people can and cannot do with your work. In the United States, this right to control your work has actually turned into big business, but that's what allows all the creative people around us to get paid for coming up with all the fantastic plays, paintings songs, television shows, books, computer games, and movies that we all enjoy and appreciate. You as the owner of a copyright are the only person who can do or authorize the following:

- Right to reproduce the work (make copies of the work)
- Right to distribute copies of the work
- Right to publicly display the work (such as artwork or material used on the internet}
- Right to publicly perform the work (such as plays, films or music)
- Right to produce derivative works (to make changes, modifications or other uses of the work)

One of the most important rights granted by the U.S. Copyright Act is the reproduction right. Under this right, **ONLY** the copyright owner can make any reproductions or copies of the work. Examples of unauthorized acts which are prohibited under this right include photocopying a book or pages of a book, copying code in a computer software program, and including parts of another's song into a new song. It is important to note that it is not required that the original work be copied in its entirety for an infringement of the reproduction right to occur. Rather, what is required is that the copying be "substantial and material."

Also, U.S. Copyright law gives the owner of a copyright the exclusive right to distribute their work. In other words, you as the copyright owner will have the exclusive right to make to sale, rent, or lease your work. This right allows the copyright holder to prevent the distribution of unauthorized copies of a work.

In the same fashion, U.S. Copyright law, allows a copyright owner exclusive control over when the work is performed "publicly." A performance is considered "public" when the work is performed in a "place open to the public or at a place where a substantial number of persons outside of a normal circle of a family and its social acquaintances are gathered." A performance is also considered to be public if it is transmitted to multiple locations, such as through television and radio.

Not only does the U.S. Copyright law grant the copyright owner the exclusive right to publicly perform the work, but it also grants the copyright owner the exclusive right to publicly display the work. The right to publicly display is similar to the right to publicly perform, except that this right controls the "display" of a work to the public.

By the same token, U.S. Copyright law grants copyright owners the exclusive right to make derivative works such as the transformation of a novel into a motion picture, translating a novel into a different language, remixing a song, or creating a second version of a software program.

As a practical matter, as an entrepreneur, startup company, or small business owner, you should identify any potential copyrights that you or your business may own. Once ascertained, you should register each and every one of them with the U.S. Copyright Office. This will give you protection over all of your business's copyrights and establish grounds for a copyright infringement lawsuit if anyone uses it without your permission.

* * *

Key Takeaways

- Copyright is automatic with the creation of an original work.

- Although registration is not required, there are economic benefits to timely registering your work with the U.S. Copyright Office.

- Copyright notice is not required but including copyright notice on your works makes it easier to claim that someone knowingly infringed your work.

- Copyright law grants exclusive rights to reproduce, distribute, publicly display, publicly perform, and make derivative works to the owner of the copyright.

« CHAPTER SEVEN »

Independent Contractors & Copyright Law

Most businesses, especially new businesses or startup companies, will most likely use independent contractors at some point. Particularly, when first starting a business independent contractors are often used to design a company's website, create images for building a brand, to create and to develop marketing material, or to develop software, etc. However what is often overlooked by entrepreneurs is that when you hire an independent contractor to design your website, create your brand, develop software etc. then the independent contractor owns the copyright in these works.

Therefore, it is critical that you, as a business owner, obtain a written assignment, or transfer, of ownership in copyrights of the works created. The agreement **MUST** be in writing. An oral agreement or oral contract between the parties is not sufficient. Therefore, it is very, very important to have a written agreement in place with any independent contractor prior to the contractor commencing work for you, with the agreement setting forth that the copyrights in the creative works will be assigned to you or your business.

Another issue involving independent contractors and copyright law that is often encountered by entrepreneurs is the "work-made-for-hire" situation. It is important to keep in mind that the term "work made for hire" is defined by statute that only covers (i) the situation of an employee creating within the scope of employment for an employer, and (ii) very specific types of works such as, tests, answer materials for tests, atlases, motion pictures, instructional texts, etc., and there must be a writing identifying the work as a "work made for hire.

This does not mean that any and all work that is performed by an independent contractor for your business needs a "work-made-for-hire" agreement. This is a very common mistake often made by entrepreneurs. Unfortunately, many new business owners wrongly assume that if they call something a "work made for hire" in an agreement, then it simply means that the hiring party will own the copyrights. This is not the case. In order to transfer ownership of copyrights from an independent contractor to your business, a written assignment, as discussed above, is what is required.

In fact, in some instances, calling something a "work made for hire" when it is not a "work made for hire" under the U.S. Copyright law can create a multitude of problems for your business. For example, under the laws of some states, defining a business relationship as a "work made for hire" means that the contractor is technically an employee of the hiring party. As a result, your business may be responsible for paying workers' compensation insurance, unemployment insurance, payroll taxes, employee benefits, social security taxes, etc. As a practical tip, there is hardly ever a reason to define something as a "work made for hire.

* * *

Key Takeaways

- Beware of "work-made-for-hire' language in an Independent Contractor agreement.

- Your company will not own the copyright in the work done by an independent contractor unless your company obtains a written assignment of copyright ownership.

- The written assignment should be included as part of the independent contractor agreement and should be signed before the independent contractor starts any work for your company.

« CHAPTER EIGHT »

Contracts, Contracts, Contracts

When it comes to protecting your company's intellectual property, all of your contracts or written agreements matter. Any and all written agreements that touch on the ownership and secrecy of your intellectual property are of great importance. Particularly, the terms and conditions of the agreements you have in place with your vendors, employees, suppliers, investors, independent contractors, etc... Far too often emerging entrepreneurs and small business owners treat such agreements as minor formalities rather than agreements that can critically impact the intellectual property rights of their business.

For example, choosing which state's laws govern the contract can greatly impact the degree of intellectual property protection your business has. Similarly, you may have a non-disclosure agreement with a specific vendor, supplier, employee, or independent contractor, but do you also have a non-competition agreement in place with them? Does your operating agreement of your business mandate that the founders assign all intellectual property to the company?

When your startup approaches investors for funding, one of the first questions they will ask you is whether your company owns the key IP assets of the business developed by founders, employees, and contractors. Therefore, it is extremely important that you solidify your business relationships with the proper written terms to protect the intellectual property of your business and prevent your sensitive information from distribution to a third party.

Following this discussion are several sample contracts to use as a guide when putting agreements in place for your business. The sample contracts are for examples only. They should not merely be duplicated without consideration of an individual's particular situation. These sample contracts are not intended to cover each and every business situation, nor can such agreements anticipate specific needs associated with your business. Beyond that, these agreements need to be properly vetted by an attorney who can draft an agreement tailored to meet your specific needs. More often than you may expect, investing a few thousand dollars early in proper written agreements can avoid hundreds of thousands of dollars in legal work involved in a lawsuit.

Key Takeaways

- Every contract signed by your company is important and must be reviewed to determine any impact the agreement may have on your company's intellectual property assets.

- Before you hire employees or independent contractors, etc. be sure to get a contract signed before any work is started.

- Pay close attention to contract provisions that interfere with your company's ability to sell, license, assign or otherwise transfer your company's intellectual property.

« CHAPTER NINE »

Sample Agreements

<u>Sample Employment Agreement</u>

This Employment Agreement ("Agreement") is made effective on _____, by and between _____ ("Employee") and _____ ("Employer").

Employee will primarily perform their job duties at _____.

Whereas Employer desires the services of Employee, and Employee is willing to be employed by Employer, the parties therefore agree as follows:

1. <u>Employment</u>. Employee shall provide the following general services: _____. Employee accepts and agrees to such employment, and agrees to be subject to the general supervision, advice and direction of _____. Employee shall also perform (i) such other duties as are customarily performed by an employee in a similar

Waukeshia D. Jackson. Esq.

position, and (ii) such other and unrelated services and duties as may be assigned to from time to time.

2. <u>Best efforts of Employee</u>. Employee agrees to perform faithfully, industriously, and to the best of their ability, experience, and talents, all of the duties that may be required by the express and implicit terms of this Agreement, to the reasonable satisfaction of Employer. Such duties shall be provided at such place(s) as the needs, business, or opportunities of business may require from time to time.

3. <u>Compensation of Employee</u>. Employee will receive an annual salary of $_____$, payable in accordance with Employer's standard payroll procedures. Upon termination of this Agreement, for any reason, payments under this paragraph shall cease; provided, however, that Employee shall be entitled to payments for periods or partial periods that occurred prior to the date of termination and for which Employee has not already been paid, and for any commission earned in accordance

with_____customary procedures, if applicable. No payment shall be made for untaken personal or vacation days. This section of the Agreement is included for accounting and payroll purposes and should not be construed as establishing a minimum or definite term of employment.

4. <u>Expense Reimbursement</u>. Employer will reimburse Employee for expenses undertaken for business purposes in accordance with its policies then in effect.

5. <u>Confidentiality</u>. Employee recognizes the importance of protecting Employer's intellectual property, trade secrets, and business knowledge. Employee will not divulge this vital information items ("Information") which are valuable, special and unique assets of Employer, and Employee further agrees that Employee will not at any time or in any manner, either directly or indirectly, divulge, disclose, or communicate any Information to any third party without Employer's prior written consent. Employee will protect the Information and treat it as strictly confidential at all

times, during and after Employee's employment ends with Employer. A violation by of this section shall be a material violation of this Agreement and will justify legal and/or equitable relief and injunction, where appropriate by Employer.

6. Unauthorized Disclosure of Information. If it appears Employee has disclosed, or threatened disclosure, of Information in violation of this Agreement, Employer shall be entitled to an injunction to restrain Employee from disclosing, in whole or in part, such Information, or from providing any services to any party to whom such Information has been disclosed or may be disclosed. Employer shall not be prohibited by this provision from pursuing other remedies, including a claim for losses and damages.

7. Confidentiality after Termination. The confidentiality provisions of this Agreement shall remain in full force and effect for all remain in effect until the Confidential

Information no longer qualifies as a trade secret or becomes publicly available.

8. <u>Non-Compete Agreement</u>. Employee recognizes that Employer Information is a special and unique asset of the company and needs to be protected from improper disclosure. In consideration of the disclosure of the Information, Employee agrees that for one (1) year following the termination of this Agreement, whether such termination is voluntary or involuntary, and Employee will not directly or indirectly engage in any business that directly or indirectly competes with Employer. This agreement shall apply to directly or indirectly engaging in any competitive business which includes, but is not limited to: (i) engaging in a business as owner, partner, or agent, (ii) becoming an employee of any third party that is engaged in such business, (iii) becoming interested directly or indirectly in any such business, or (iv) soliciting any customer of Employer _____for the benefit of a third party that is engaged in such business. Employee agrees that this non-compete provision will not adversely affect employee's livelihood and waives any right

to make any such claim in the future. If there are geographic limits to this Section, they should be listed here: _____. If none appear, the Agreement will presume none are applicable in the eyes of both Employee and Employer and this Section should be construed accordingly by any court of competent jurisdiction. Furthermore, Employee shall be responsible to show any prospective new employer during this one year time period this provision of this Agreement, to reduce the likelihood of that Employer causing Employee to violate this Agreement.

9. <u>Employee Inability to Contract for Employer</u>. Employee shall not have the right to make any contracts or commitments for or on behalf of Employer_____without first obtaining the express written consent of Employer.

10. <u>Benefits, Holidays, Insurance, Personal Leave and Vacation</u>. Employee shall be entitled to these according to the Employer's policies in effect at the time.

11. **Term and Termination.** Employee's employment under this Agreement shall be for an unspecified term on an "at will" basis. Either party may terminate this Agreement at any time and without cause. Violation of this Agreement will terminate employment without notice and with no compensation, except for that due up to such date of termination.

12. **Compliance with Employer Rules, Policies, and Procedures.** Employee agrees to comply with all of the rules and regulations of Employer, and understands that these rules will change from time to time, and Employee must continue to abide by them in order to continue employment with Employer.

13. **Return of Property.** Upon termination of this Agreement, Employee shall deliver to Employer all property, which is property or related to Employer's business (including keys, records, notes, data, models,

laptops, printers, cell phones and all other equipment) that is in Employee's possession, custody, or control.

14. <u>Notices</u>. Any notice required by this Agreement or given in connection with it, shall be in writing and shall be given to the appropriate party by personal delivery or a recognized overnight delivery service such as FedEx.

If to Employee:_____ (Employee Address).

If to Employer:_____ (Employer Address).

15. <u>No Waiver</u>. The waiver or failure of either party to exercise in any respect any right provided in this agreement shall not be deemed a waiver of any other right or remedy to which the party may be entitled.

16. <u>Entirety of Agreement</u>. The terms and conditions set forth herein constitute the entire agreement between the parties and supersede any communications or previous agreements with respect to the subject matter of this Agreement. There are no written or oral understandings

directly or indirectly related to this Agreement that are not set forth herein. No change can be made to this Agreement other than in writing and signed by both parties.

17. <u>Governing Law</u>. This Agreement shall be construed and enforced according to the laws of the State of _____ and any dispute under this Agreement must be brought in this venue and no other.

18. <u>Headings in this Agreement</u>   The headings in this Agreement are for convenience only, confirm no rights or obligations in either party, and do not alter any terms of this Agreement.

19. <u>Severability</u>. If any term of this Agreement is held by a court of competent jurisdiction to be invalid or unenforceable, then this Agreement, including all of the remaining terms, will remain in full force and effect as if such invalid or unenforceable term had never been included.

In Witness whereof, the parties have executed this Agreement as of the date first written above.

_____
Employee

_____
Employer

_____
Date

<u>Sample Employee Non-Compete Agreement</u>

_____, referred to as EMPLOYEE, and ____, referred to as COMPANY, agree:

_____ is employed by ____ as _____. EMPLOYEE and COMPANY acknowledge that as a result of the employer/employee relationship existing that EMPLOYEE will from time to time receive, or create confidential information related to trade secrets, customer lists, vendor lists, business plans, processes, procedures, designs, systems and that such information might be useful to competitors.

Upon termination of employment by COMPANY, EMPLOYEE shall not accept employment in any capacity, act as proprietor, shareholder or act as an independent contractor for any _____COMPANY located within a radius of ____ miles from the center of the city of license of the COMPANY, for a period of ____ years.

The parties agree that the damages, which may be suffered by COMPANY upon violation of this agreement, are irreparable and intangible in nature. Therefore, the parties agree that COMPANY shall be entitled to injunctive relief to enforce this agreement.

The parties agree that all disputes related to this agreement shall be arbitrated under the rules of the American Arbitration Association, before a single arbiter. The decision of the arbiter shall be final, and may be entered by any Court of competent jurisdiction as a final judgment.

The prevailing party in any dispute related to his agreement shall be entitled to its reasonable counsel fees.

This is the entire agreement between the parties, and this agreement may only be modified in writing executed by both parties.

Dated: _____

_____
EMPLOYEE

_____
COMPANY by an authorized officer

`Sample Independent Contractor Agreement

This agreement is made as of the date last indicated below between _____ (the "Company"), a _____ (TYPE OF BUSINESS ENTITY) under the laws of _____ with a principal place of business at _____, and _____ (the "Independent Contractor"), with a home address of: _____.

WHEREAS the Company and the Independent Contractor wish to enter into this Independent Contractor Agreement ("Agreement") governing the terms and conditions of the contract.

THIS AGREEMENT WITNESSETH that in consideration of the premises and mutual covenants and agreements hereinafter contained and for other good and valuable consideration (the receipt and sufficiency of which is hereby acknowledged by the parties hereto), it is agreed by and between the parties hereto as follows:

1. **Scope of Services:** The Independent Contractor will perform the duties of _____for the

rates of pay outlined in Schedule "A" of this Agreement. The Company may change the scope of services at its sole discretion and for business reasons. In carrying out these duties and responsibilities, the Independent Contractor shall comply with all policies, procedures, rules, and regulations, both written and oral, as are announced by The Company.

2. **Compensation:** Compensation is outlined in Schedule "A" of this agreement.

3. **<u>Relationship of the Parties</u>.** Independent Contractor enters into this Agreement as, and shall continue to be, an independent contractor. All Services shall be performed only by Independent Contractor. Under no circumstances shall Contractor, look to Company as his/her employer, or as a partner, agent or principal. Independent Contractor shall be solely responsible for any and all taxes, Social Security contributions or payments, disability insurance, unemployment taxes, and other

payroll type taxes applicable to such compensation. Independent Contractor hereby indemnifies and holds Company harmless from, any claims, losses, costs, fees, liabilities, damages or injuries suffered by Company arising out of Independent Contractor's failure with respect to its obligations in this Section 3. The Independent Contractor agrees that as an independent contractor, the Independent Contractor will not be qualified to participate in or to receive any employee benefits that the Company may extend to its employees.

4. **Intellectual Property**: The Independent Contractor agrees that without limitation, any documents, patents, trademarks copyright, trade secrets, know-how, processes or other intellectual property created or improved by the Independent Contractor during the term of this Agreement, shall be exclusive property of the Company. The Independent Contractor agrees to execute, from time to time, upon request by the Company, assignments of his or her rights in any intellectual property as noted above to

the Company, and shall cooperate with the Company in documenting the ownership of such intellectual property by the Company. The Independent Contractor also hereby waives his or her moral rights to such intellectual property at common law and under the *Copyright Act.*

5. **Confidentiality:** It is understood that during the course of this Agreement, the Independent Contractor will acquire and be exposed to information about certain matters which are confidential to the Company and not known to the public or to competitors and which information is the exclusive property of the Company. By agreeing to the terms of this Agreement, the Independent Contractor acknowledges that such confidential information could be used to the detriment of the Company. Accordingly, the Independent Contractor shall keep confidential at any time during or after the term of this Agreement, any information about the business and affairs of, or belonging to, the Company, its customers or suppliers, including without

limitation information relating to pricing, customer identity, technical data, and market information. Further, after the termination of employment with the Company, regardless of how that termination should occur, the Independent Contractor hereby undertakes, without time limitation, not to disclose to any third party and to treat in strict confidence all confidential information referred to above, except where disclosure is made with the prior written consent of the Company and where third party has executed a confidentiality agreement with Company.

6. **Non-Competition**: The Independent Contractor agrees that he or she shall not, during the term of this Agreement and for a period of _____years from the date of the termination of this Agreement for any reason, in the directly or indirectly or in any other manner whatsoever, carry on or be engaged in or be interested in a business which provides for _____services of the kind that the Company has the ability to provide. Further, the Independent Contractor will not permit his or her

name, or any part thereof, to be used by or employed by any person or business involved in providing _____ services of the kind that the Company has the ability to provide.

7. **Non-Solicitation of Independent Contractors**: During the during the term of this Agreement and for a period of _____ years following the termination of this Agreement, the Independent Contractor will not hire or take away or cause to be hired or taken away, any Independent Contractors or employees of the Company.

8. **Non-Solicitation of Customers**: For a period of _____ years following the termination of this Agreement, the Independent Contractor will not directly or indirectly solicit business from any client or customer or potential client or customer of the Company which was serviced or solicited by the Company during the course of employment. The Independent Contractor shall have no rights to the Company's client or employees list after termination.

9. **Acknowledgment:** The Independent Contractor hereby acknowledges and agrees that the time limitations in sections 8, 9 and 10 are reasonable and properly required for the adequate protection of the property and business of the Company.

10. **Termination:** This Agreement may be terminated as follows:

    (i) By the Company, at any time, for just cause, without providing the Independent Contractor with termination pay, reasonable notice or pay in lieu thereof.

    Just cause includes but is not limited to:

    (a) A material breach of any of the provisions of this Offer of Employment.

> (b) Non-compliance with policies, procedures and operating guidelines of the Company.
>
> (c) Theft, fraud or willful misconduct.

(ii) The Independent Contractor may terminate this Agreement, at any time and for any reason whatsoever, upon giving the Company_____) weeks prior written notice.

11. **Authorized Deductions:** The Independent Contractor hereby authorizes the Company to deduct from any payment due to the Independent Contractor at any time, including from termination payment, any amounts owed to the Company by reason of purchases, advances or loans or pursuant to the terms of this Agreement.

12. **Assignment**: The terms and provisions of this Agreement shall endure to the benefit of the Company and its successors and assigns. The terms

of this Agreement may be assigned by the Company at its sole discretion.

13. **Severability:** In the event that any provision or part of this Agreement is deemed invalid by a court, the remaining provisions, or parts thereof, shall remain in full force and effect. This Agreement, and the policies referred within it, constitutes the entire agreement between the Company and the Independent Contractor. This Agreement shall be governed by and construed in accordance with the laws of the State of Georgia.

14. **Legal Advice:** The Independent Contractor is encouraged to seek legal advice with respect to the terms of this Agreement. By signing this document, the Independent Contractor acknowledges that he or she understands the terms of this Agreement and has had the opportunity to seek and obtain independent legal advice with regard to the execution of this Agreement and the meaning of the provisions contained within it.

Waukeshia D. Jackson. Esq.

I have read, understand, and agree with the above.

_____
Independent Contractor Signature
_____
Date

SCHEDULE "A"

The Independent Contractor will perform the following role of _____outlined in Schedule "A".

_____: The Independent Contractor shall be paid (t less all applicable statutory deductions and withholdings.

The Independent Contractor shall perform the following duties:

_____

_____

_____

<u>Sample Non-Disclosure Agreement</u>

This Non-Disclosure Agreement ("Agreement") is made and entered into this _____ day of _____, 2017, j by and between: _____, as an individual or affiliated companies ("Receiving Party") AND_____, as an individual or affiliated companies ("Disclosing Party").

WHEREAS, Disclosing Party has Confidential Information in the form of invention description(s), technical and business information or material relating to proprietary ideas and inventions, copyrights, trademarks trade secrets, drawings and/or illustrations, patent searches, existing and/or contemplated products and services, research and development, production, costs, profit and margin information, finances and financial projections, customers, clients, marketing, and current or future business plans and models, regardless of whether such information is designated as "Confidential Information" at the time of its disclosure.

WHEREAS, Receiving Party shall use the Confidential Information only for the purposes of_____.

NOW, **THEREFORE**, for good and valuable consideration, the receipt and sufficiency which are hereby acknowledged, Receiving Party agrees as follows:

1. Receiving Party acknowledges that all Confidential Information is confidential and proprietary to Disclosing Party. The term Confidential Information does not include information that (i) is already in Receiving Party's possession (other than information previously furnished to the Receiving Party by the Disclosing Party or its agents), provided that such information is not known by Receiving Party to be subject to another agreement or obligation of confidentiality, or (ii) becomes generally

available to the public other than the result of a disclosure by the Receiving Party or (iii) becomes available to Receiving Party on a non-confidential basis from a source other than Disclosing Party or its agents or advisors, provided that such source is not bound by an agreement or other obligation of confidentiality. Receiving Party shall keep all such information confidential and shall not, expect as may be required by law, disclose, summarize or otherwise provide any or all of the Confidential Information in any manner.

2. Receiving Party agrees for a period of _____ years from the date of this Agreement, not to use any of the Confidential Information to compete with the Disclosing Party.

3. Receiving Party may not disclose or otherwise provide any portion of the Confidential Information to any third party. Receiving party shall hold Confidential Information in confidence until the Confidential Information becomes publicly available.

4. Upon any request by Disclosing Party or upon termination of Disclosing Party's relationship with Receiving Party, Receiving Party shall promptly return to Disclosing Party all Confidential Information received.

5. Receiving Party shall not, without prior written approval of Disclosing Party, use for Receiving Party's own benefit, publish, copy, or otherwise disclose to others, or permit the use by others for their benefit or to the detriment of Disclosing Party, any Confidential Information. Receiving Party shall return to Disclosing Party any and all records, notes, and other written, printed, or tangible materials in its possession pertaining to Confidential Information immediately if Disclosing Party requests it in writing.

6. This Agreement shall be governed by and construed in accordance with the laws of the State of_____, without regard to principles of choice of law or conflicts of law. Each party

further agrees that, for purposes of jurisdiction and venue, any action regarding this Agreement will be in the Supreme Court of _____ County, _____. In the event of a dispute concerning this Agreement, the prevailing party shall be entitled to recover its reasonable attorneys' fees and other costs and expenses incurred in connection with such dispute.

7. The person signing this document on behalf of the Receiving Party represents and warrants that the Receiving Party has duly authorized this Agreement and that he or she has the authority to sign on behalf of the Receiving Party.

8. This Agreement shall be binding on the Receiving Party's representatives, successors and assigns and shall insure to the benefit of the Disclosing Party's heirs, representatives, successors and assigns.

9. Nothing contained in this Agreement shall be deemed to constitute either party a partner, joint

venture or employee of the other party for any purpose.

10. If a court finds any provision of this Agreement invalid or unenforceable, the remainder of this Agreement shall be interpreted so as best to affect the intent of the parties.

11. This Agreement expresses the complete understanding of the parties with respect to the subject matter and supersedes all prior proposals, agreements, representations, and understandings. This Agreement may not be amended except in a writing signed by both parties.

12. The failure to exercise any right provided in this Agreement shall not be a waiver of prior or subsequent rights.

Disclosing Party	Receiving Party
By: _____	By: _____
Printed Name: _____	Printed Name: _____
Title: _____	Title: _____
Dated: _____	Dated: _____

Sample Trademark License Agreement

This Trademark License Agreement ("the Agreement") is made and is effective on as of _____, 20_____ ("Effective Date") by and between _____as an individual or affiliated companies (the "Licensor") and _____ as an individual or affiliated companies (the "Licensee") The Licensor and the Licensee may be referred to individually as a "Party" or collectively as the "

WHEREAS the Parties agree as follows:

LICENSOR owns the rights and trademark registrations to certain characteristic designs, trade names, trademarks, service marks, logos, and other proprietary information which are associated with it, its activities, or its property. A list of these items (collectively "the MARKS") is attached to this agreement as Exhibit One. LICENSEE acknowledges the LICENSOR's rights in and to these MARKS in connection with its wholesale manufacturing and merchandising

Waukeshia D. Jackson. Esq.

business; the LICENSOR is willing to grant such a license, upon the terms contained in this Agreement.

LICENSOR grants to LICENSEE an exclusive license to use the MARKS in connection with LICENSEE's merchandising business with respect to the following items ("items") and no others:

_____ in the following territories, and no others:

_____

This license shall authorize LICENSEE to reproduce and use the symbols on those items in accordance with the terms of this Agreement.

LICENSEE'S INTEREST.

LICENSEE acknowledges that nothing in this Agreement grants to LICENSEE any right title or interest in any of the

MARKS licensed hereunder, except the right to use such MARK as provided in this agreement.

TERM. This license shall be effective from the date of this Agreement through _____, and shall then expire unless renewed.

ROYALTIES

(a) Rate of Royalty. In consideration of the license granted to it, LICENSEE shall pay to the LICENSOR a royalty equal to _____ percent, which rate may be adjusted as is provided below, of its wholesale price (without any adjustment for volume or other discounts) of all items sold by it using the MARKS. For purposes of this Agreement, an item shall be considered "sold" upon the date of billing, invoicing, shipping, or payment, whichever occurs first.

(b) Minimum Payments. Notwithstanding subparagraph (a) above, as minimum payments under this Agreement, LICENSEE shall be required to remit $____ (_____ & _____/100 dollars) to the LICENSOR upon execution of this

Agreement. This advance payment will be applied to royalty payments due herein.

PAYMENT

All payments required by Licensee hereunder shall be made to Licensor in _____ (STATE) in U.S. Dollars, and all references to dollars throughout this Agreement shall mean U.S. Dollars. - Payment of the royalties shall be due quarterly for the three-month periods ending on the last day of each calendar quarter and the period ending on the last day of this Agreement if other than such a quarterly period. Payment shall be in good funds not later than 30 days after the close of each quarterly period or last day covering all sales which occurred during the period.

Payment shall be accompanied by an accounting acceptable in form to the LICENSOR showing all sales which occurred during the period including, but not limited to, the type of item, the wholesale price, the quantity, the name and address of the purchaser, and the computation of royalty due. The first royalty payment shall be due no later than _____. In the event of any late payment, LICENSEE shall pay interest at the rate of 12 percent per annum from the 30th day after the end of each calendar quarter until the date of payment.

AUDIT

Licensee shall, at its sole cost and expense, maintain complete and accurate books and records (specifically including, without limitation, the originals or copies of documents supporting entries in the books of account) covering all transactions arising out of or relating to this Agreement. In addition, Licensor and its duly authorized representative have the right, during normal business hours, for the duration of this Agreement and for_____ years thereafter, to examine and copy said books and records and all other documents and materials in the possession of and under the control of Licensee with respect to the subject matter and terms of this Agreement. In the event a sublicense is approved by Licensor as provided hereunder, Licensee shall also obtain for Licensor the right in any and all of such sublicenses for Licensor to similarly inspect the books and records of the sub licensees. The exercise by Licensor of any right to audit at any time or times or the acceptance by Licensor of any statement, or payment shall be without prejudice to any of Licensor's rights or remedies and shall not bar Licensor from thereafter disputing the accuracy of any payment or statement and Licensee shall remain fully liable for any balance due under this Agreement.

APPROVAL

LICENSOR shall have the right at all reasonable times to inspect the items employing the MARKS to ensure that such use is of proper quality and otherwise consistent with this Agreement. LICENSEE shall not use the symbols in any manner derogatory or otherwise unacceptable to the LICENSOR.

NO ALTERATIONS. LICENSEE shall use the symbols only as developed and approved by the LICENSOR. LICENSEE shall not alter the MARKS in any way without first obtaining the LICENSOR's express written consent.

EXPLOITATION

LICENSEE shall use its best efforts to exploit the MARKS so as to maximize sales of items using the symbols while at the same time preserving the high standards of the LICENSOR. Without limiting the generality of the preceding sentence, LICENSEE shall maintain sufficient inventories of or manufacturing capability for items using the MARKS so as to be able to fill promptly all purchase orders including but not limited to purchase orders from the LICENSOR. All items using the MARKS shall be of high quality, design, and workmanship, and shall contain the notation "Manufactured under license from_____ LICENSOR." The parties recognize that, notwithstanding their relationship as independent contractors, any inferior items will reflect unfavorably on the LICENSOR. Therefore, LICENSEE shall not use any promotional, packing, or other materials or items in connection with items using the symbols which may reflect adversely upon the LICENSOR or to which the LICENSOR shall object.

ADDITIONAL INFORMATION

LICENSEE shall furnish such additional information pertaining to sales of items using the symbols as the LICENSOR may reasonably request. This shall include, but not be limited to, information necessary or helpful to the LICENSOR to protect its rights with respect to the MARKS.'

SUB-LICENSES, TRANSFERS, ETC.

The license provided for in this Agreement is granted solely to LICENSEE. LICENSEE may not grant any sub-licenses nor may it transfer the license or any interest in it to others, either by operation of law or otherwise.

INFRINGEMENT

The LICENSOR shall be responsible at its expense for defending the MARKS from infringement by others and defending against any claims by others that the MARKS infringe upon their rights, all as the LICENSOR may determine in its sole discretion. LICENSOR shall defend indemnify, and hold harmless LICENSEE from any such claims of infringement by others. Upon any claims of infringement, LICENSEE shall promptly comply with the LICENSOR's instructions concerning the allegedly infringing item including, but not limited to, ceasing immediately all further sales of the item. LICENSEE shall promptly notify the LICENSOR of any possible infringement or claim of infringement of which it becomes aware.

PRODUCT LIABILITY.

LICENSEE shall be solely responsible for the design and manufacture of the items to which the MARKS will be applied and for the manner of application of the symbols to the items. Should any product liability claims arise with respect to any such item, LICENSEE shall be solely responsible for them and shall defend with competent counsel, indemnify, and hold harmless the LICENSOR from any liability with respect to such claims.

INSURANCE.

LICENSEE shall maintain during the term of this Agreement liability insurance (including product liability coverage) in form, amount, and coverage reasonably satisfactory to the LICENSOR to protect against any loss of the kind contemplated by the preceding paragraph. LICENSEE shall provide the LICENSOR with evidence of such insurance, including a certificate naming the LICENSOR as an additional insured under the policy. LICENSEE shall obtain the written acknowledgment of its insurance carrier that LICENSEE's insurance shall be primary with respect to any loss contemplated by the policy. The insurance shall provide that the LICENSOR must be given at least 30 days written notice before LICENSEE's insurance can be reduced, canceled, or not renewed.

TERMINATION

Should LICENSEE default with respect to any of its obligations under this Agreement, the LICENSOR may terminate this Agreement by written notice to LICENSEE, and the license and all of LICENSEE's rights under this Agreement shall then immediately cease. Notwithstanding the preceding, upon any such termination LICENSEE may, for a period of 120 days after the termination sell upon the terms of this Agreement and through normal distribution channels any items using the symbols which it may have in inventory or in process at the time of termination.

INDEPENDENT CONTRACTOR

The parties to this Agreement shall be independent contractors and shall have no other relationship not expressly granted by this Agreement. Neither shall hold itself out as having any other relationship to the other, and upon request from the other a party shall furnish a written disclaimer as to any other relationship. Neither party shall have the power or the right to bind or create liability for the other by its intentional or negligent act. Each shall defend with competent counsel, indemnify, and hold harmless the other for all claims of any kind arising out of its own acts or failures to act.

ENTIRE AGREEMENT

This Agreement contains the entire understanding of the parties with respect to its subject matter and supersedes all prior negotiations and understandings of every kind.

This Agreement is established as of the date set forth below by the following signatures of the parties.

Date: _____

_____

LICENSOR

_____

LICENSEE

« CHAPTER TEN »

FINAL THOUGHTS

I co-founded Jackson & Lowe Law Group, P.C. in the spring of 2014 without a single client. Today, I have a successful intellectual property law practice aimed at providing aspiring entrepreneurs, inventors, and small business owners with insights into the legal landscape associated with starting a business. Through this book, my goals are to inspire people and organizations to develop their ideas whether it is through developing and patenting their inventions, building and establishing their brands through trademarks, securing rights to their creative works through copyright or creating contracts to establish and enforce their business practices and business relationships.

As an entrepreneur myself, I understand the importance of creating value for your clients and customers. Therefore, I hope that that there is at least some information provided in this book that you can use as an entrepreneur to be successful in your innovative pursuits. My final thought to anyone who has read this book is to keep in mind that every business is different. Therefore, there may be other items you need to address your specific business goals and concerns. So, be sure to speak to an attorney about your business to ensure all your bases are covered before securing any future clients/customers with an agreement.

www.ingramcontent.com/pod-product-compliance
Lightning Source LLC
Chambersburg PA
CBHW021411170526
45164CB00002B/596